IS AMERICA IN BIBLE PROPHECY?

MARK HITCHCOCK

Multnomah Books

IS AMERICA IN BIBLE PROPHECY?
published by Multnomah Books

© 2002 by Mark Hitchcock

International Standard Book Number: 978-1-57673-496-4

Cover design by Kirk DouPonce/UDG DesignWorks
Cover images by Corbis
Lower right-hand image by Getty Source

Unless otherwise indicated, Scripture quotations are from:
New American Standard Bible® © 1960, 1977, 1995
by the Lockman Foundation. Used by permission.

Other Scripture quotations:
Holy Bible, New Living Translation (NLT) © 1996. Used by permission of Tyndale
House Publishers, Inc. All rights reserved. *The Holy Bible,* New International Version
(NIV) © 1973, 1984 by International Bible Society, used by permission of Zondervan
Publishing House *The Holy Bible,* King James Version (KJV)

Published in the United States by WaterBrook Multnomah, an imprint of the Crown
Publishing Group, a division of Random House Inc., New York.

MULTNOMAH and its mountain colophon are registered trademarks of Random
House Inc.

Printed in the United States of America

For information:
MULTNOMAH BOOKS
12265 ORACLE BOULEVARD, SUITE 200 • COLORADO SPRINGS, CO 80921

Library of Congress Cataloging-in-Publication Data
Hitchcock, Mark.
    Is America in Bible prophecy? / by Mark Hitchcock.
        p. cm.
Includes bibliographical references.
    ISBN 1-57673-496-X (pbk.)
    1. Bible--Prophecies--United States. 2. United States--History--Prophecies.
    3. Bible--Prophecies--End of the world. 4. End of the world--Biblical
teaching. I. Title.
    BS649.U6 H58 2002
    220.1'5--dc21   2002001068

09—10 9 8 7

CONTENTS

INTRODUCTION

I have to confess: I love Bible prophecy and I love America. So I guess it was just a matter of time before I wrote a book about America in Bible prophecy. Ever since I became interested in Bible prophecy, I have wondered about the end-times destiny of the land that I love. And I've discovered that I'm not alone.

As I have had the privilege of speaking at prophecy conferences and churches over the last ten years, probably the number one question I have heard is this: Is America in Bible prophecy? Something inside us wants to know what will ultimately happen to this great land we call the United States of America.

And interest in this already popular subject has surged in recent months because of the terrorist attacks against America. In the days after the attacks, I was asked this question dozens of times.

I'd guess that at one time or another since September 11, 2001, you, too, have wondered where we are headed as a nation. You have probably asked yourself questions like these: Does the Word of God have anything to say about America in the last days? What will happen to America in the end times? How do we fit into God's prophetic program? Will America be destroyed by a nuclear attack? Will America collapse as a result of moral corruption? Will bioterrorism destroy us?

When you think about it, our interest in America's role in the prophecies about the end of the world could be interpreted as a little self-centered. After all, you rarely hear someone wondering about the end-times role of India, Scotland, Australia, Mexico, or Brazil. Don't the people in these nations matter to God as much as Americans?

Despite the fact that people in other countries might consider it a bit arrogant, I believe it is completely legitimate to wonder what will become of America in the end times. The United States is the most powerful nation in the history of the world. What's going to happen to it?

The purpose of this book is to take a concise yet in-depth look at all the theories concerning America in the last days, examine the biblical passages that are used to support these views, and then set forth what I believe is the most likely biblical scenario for the future of America.

In this book I am going to assume that the reader has at least a basic knowledge of events in the end times. To make sure you understand these events, let's do a brief review and define a few key terms that you will see sprinkled throughout the book.

THE RAPTURE OF THE CHURCH TO HEAVEN

This next event on God's prophetic timetable is the Rapture. This is when all people, living or dead, who have personally trusted in Jesus Christ as their Savior will be caught up in the air to meet the Lord and go with Him up to heaven and then return with Him to earth at least seven years later, at His second coming (see John 14:1–3; 1 Corinthians 15:50–58; 1 Thessalonians 4:13–18).

THE SEVEN-YEAR TRIBULATION PERIOD

The Tribulation is the final seven years of this age. It will begin with a peace treaty between Israel and the Antichrist and end with the second coming of Christ to earth (not to be confused with the Rapture). During these seven years, the Lord will pour out His wrath upon the earth in successive waves of judgment. But the Lord will also pour out His grace during this time by saving millions of people (read Revelation 6–19).

THE THREE-AND-A-HALF-YEAR WORLD EMPIRE OF THE ANTICHRIST

In the last half of the Tribulation, the Antichrist will rule the world politically, economically, and religiously. The entire world will either give allegiance to him or suffer persecution and death (see Revelation 13:1–18).

THE CAMPAIGN
OF ARMAGEDDON

The campaign or war of Armageddon is the final event of the Great Tribulation. In this war, all the armies of the earth will gather against Israel and attempt to eradicate the Jewish people once and for all (see Revelation 14:19–20; 16:12–16; 19:19–21).

THE SECOND COMING
OF CHRIST TO EARTH

The climactic event of human history is the literal, physical, visible, glorious return of Jesus Christ back to planet earth to destroy the armies of the world gathered in Israel and to set up His kingdom on earth, a kingdom that will last for one thousand years (see Revelation 19:11–21).

God's Blueprint for the End Times

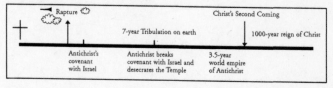

My prayer is that God will use this book in your life to give you a greater love for Bible prophecy and—most importantly—for the Savior who is its focus.

Maranatha!
"Our Lord, Come!"
May God richly bless America.

MARK HITCHCOCK

ONE NATION UNDER GOD

For thirteen years of our lives, the first thing we did every morning at school was to recite the Pledge of Allegiance to the American flag. In this pledge we boldly recall the heritage of our nation and declare that the United States is "one nation under God."

But the truth is that all nations are under God. All the nations of the earth—and their leaders—are under the sovereign hand of God.

Very early in the pages of the Bible, Scripture makes this abundantly clear: "When the Most High gave the nations their inheritance, when He separated the sons of man, He set the boundaries of the peoples according to the number of the sons of Israel" (Deuteronomy 32:8).

Job says, "He makes the nations great, then destroys them; He enlarges the nations, then leads them away" (12:23). And King David, the greatest ruler of Israel, acknowledged the rule of God over all the heavens and earth:

> "Blessed are You, O LORD God of Israel our father, forever and ever. Yours, O LORD, is the greatness and the power and the glory and the victory and the majesty, indeed everything that is in the heavens and the earth; Yours is the dominion, O LORD, and You exalt Yourself as head over all. Both riches and honor come from You, and You rule over all, and in Your hand is power and might; and it lies in Your hand to make great and to strengthen everyone." (1 Chronicles 29:10b–12)

In the book of Daniel, God reminded the great king of Babylon, Nebuchadnezzar, that it is He who rules over man's kingdoms:

"Let the name of God be blessed forever and ever, for wisdom and power belong to Him. It is He who changes the times and the epochs; He removes kings and establishes kings; He gives wisdom to wise men and knowledge to men of understanding." (Daniel 2:20–21)

"In order that the living may know that the Most High is ruler over the realm of mankind, and bestows it on whom He wishes and sets over it the lowliest of men." (Daniel 4:17b)

"For His dominion is an everlasting dominion, and His kingdom endures from generation to generation. All the inhabitants of the earth are accounted as nothing, but He does according to His will in the host of heaven and among the inhabitants of earth; and no one can ward off His hand or say to Him, 'What have You done?'" (Daniel 4:34b–35)

Later, in the first century A.D., the apostle Paul reminded the inhabitants of the mighty city of Athens that *all* the nations of the earth are under God. During his second missionary journey, Paul arrived in Athens and was overcome by the idolatry in the city. On Mars Hill he reminded the Athenians of the most important truth for any group of people to understand: God is the Creator of all things and has determined when they will rise, when they will fall, and where the exact boundaries of their expansion will be:

> "He is the God who made the world and everything in it.... He himself gives life and breath to everything, and he satisfies every need there is. From one man he created all the nations throughout the whole earth. He decided beforehand which should rise and fall, and he determined their boundaries." (Acts 17:24–26, NLT)

Why did God do this? Paul answers: "His purpose in all of this was that the nations should seek after God and perhaps feel their way toward him and find him— though he is not far from any one of us. For in him we live and move and exist" (Acts 17:27–28a, NLT).

Can you imagine preaching this message to Alexander the Great? "Sorry, Alexander, but you're not the one in charge here. God is!" How do you think Napoleon would've liked it? Or Hitler or Saddam Hussein? How about affluent America: Does she really believe she's "under God" and His authority?

Telling proud people that the God of heaven has already determined the limits of their expansion, the extent of their influence in the world, and the duration of their existence in world affairs is not going to win you any friends.[1] But it is true. God is sovereign over individuals and nations. He is Lord of all.

OUR GOD REIGNS

Ray Stedman, noted pastor and author, once traveled to England to speak at a Bible conference. The church sanctuary was filled with people eager to hear this well-known teacher. The service began with singing and praise to the Lord. One of the songs was the chorus "Our God Reigns."

Stedman, seated on the platform next to the pastor, glanced down at the song sheet and began to smile. Then he started to laugh. The words on the song sheet had been mistyped. The congregation was belting out "Our God *Resigns*."[2]

That's one of those funny-but-painful stories, isn't it? Sometimes we look at the world around us and conclude that God must have resigned and is no longer seated on His throne, ruling the nations.

We need to remind ourselves that God is indeed enthroned in heaven, reigning over all. And we must never forget that God is still on His throne, ruling over the nations of the world.

GOD OF THE NATIONS

Since God rules over all, He determines the existence and destiny of the nations of this world. And although the Bible does not give us information about many of the nations in history and in prophecy, it does clearly discuss the final destiny of many of them. At least fifteen specific nations can find their futures in the pages of Scripture as clearly as if they were in a history book:

- Israel
- Jordan (Ammon, Moab, and Edom)
- Egypt

- Sudan (Cush)
- Russia (Rosh)
- Iran (Persia)
- Iraq (Babylon)
- Europe (reunited Roman Empire)
- Central Asia (Magog)
- Syria
- Greece
- Saudi Arabia (Sheba and Dedan)
- Libya (Put)
- Lebanon (Tyre)
- Turkey

"OH, SAY CAN YOU SEE"

God is in control of each nation's destiny. He has a plan for each one. This is true of the United States as well. So what is God's prophetic plan for our nation? To borrow a phrase from a familiar patriotic tune, "Oh, say can you see" America in Bible prophecy?

Charles Ryrie, a noted theologian, poignantly addresses this question in his book *The Best Is Yet to Come:*

Nations rise and nations fall. It is a two-way street.

The might of ancient Babylon lasted only 86 years.

The powerful Persian Empire did better—208 years.

The glory of Greece was eclipsed after 268 years.

Mighty Rome ruled for almost 9 centuries.

The British Empire endured for about 250 years.

The United States of America has celebrated her bicentennial. If we make it to a tricentennial, we will beat the averages.

Now the fourth largest country in the world, both in area and population, the United States was largely a wilderness three hundred years ago. But thousands came from many lands and varied backgrounds to forge a nation that has blessed its people with the highest standard of living in the world. Rich in natural resources, technology, educational opportunities, and culture, our country seems invincible. Yet the great oil embargo of 1974 disrupted many areas of life and demonstrated our nation's vulnerability. Military experts warn that other nations are capable of destroying our major cities at the push of a button. No longer does the United States excel in all phases of military power. What lies ahead for this great country?[3]

Thomas Ice and Timothy Demy also note the importance of this question.

"God bless America!" Is it a prayer, a promise, or a prophecy? We can see and hear the slogan in music, on bumper stickers, in casual conversations, in campaign rhetoric, at historic moments in our nation's life (both joyful and sorrowful), from podiums, in parades, and in a host of other public and religious forums. Will God bless the United States in the future? Is there any sure word of our nation's future in the Bible generally, and the prophetic passages specifically? It's amazing!

One of the most frequently asked questions we receive is with regard to the role of the United States in Bible prophecy. Is it fact or fantasy?[4]

Every prophecy teacher or writer I know of would admit that America, like most nations, is not mentioned *by name* anywhere in the pages of Scripture. This is obvious. Nevertheless, America is clearly a part of the general framework of prophecy. Numerous passages in the Bible refer to God's final dealings with "all the nations." Most would agree that America is included in such general references in Scripture.

However, the real question is this: Do specific passages in Scripture chronicle the role of America in the last days without giving the exact name "America" or "the United States"? Many students of Bible prophecy believe so.

In the next three chapters, I want us to take a look at the key passages of prophetic Scripture that people have said refer to America.

IS AMERICA BABYLON THE GREAT?

S ince the recent terrorist attacks on America, I have heard this question over and over again. People want to know if America (and specifically New York City) is Babylon the great as referred to in Revelation 17–18.

I heard a prophecy teacher say just this on television. He claimed that New York City is the Babylon of Revelation and that the fall of the World Trade Center was a fulfillment of Bible prophecy. To support his conclusion, he cited Revelation 18:9–11:

"And the kings of the earth, who committed acts of immorality and lived sensuously with her, will weep and lament over her when they see the smoke of her burning, standing at a distance because of the fear of her torment, saying, 'Woe, woe, the great city, Babylon, the strong city! For in one hour your judgment has come.' And the merchants of the earth weep and mourn over her, because no one buys their cargoes any more."

This preacher went on to vividly describe how New York City is the great commercial capital of the world, how the whole world could see the smoke of her burning on September 11, how the merchants wept over the city, and how she was destroyed in "one hour."

This interpretation makes for good television, but there are many problems with this position. The most obvious is that Revelation says that God destroys Babylon at the end of the seven-year tribulation period, just before Jesus' second coming to defeat Antichrist's armies at Armageddon. Since none of that has happened, not many people would say that

September 11, 2001, was the end of the Tribulation.

So although we may set aside the notion that the terrorist attacks on the World Trade Center were the fulfillment of Revelation 18–19, we must still deal with the theory that the Babylon of Revelation 18–19 is America or New York City.

MAKING THE CASE

One of the key individuals who believes that America is Babylon is S. Franklin Logsdon. He finds it inconceivable that God would not mention America in Scripture:

> It would be most unwise to declare that the U.S.A. is not in prophecy, that the Lord did not see these conditions existing here as well as in the other nations of the world.
>
> Actually, it is unthinkable that the God who knows the end from the beginning would pinpoint such small nations as Libya, Egypt, Ethiopia and Syria in the prophetic declaration and completely overlook the wealthiest and most powerful nation on the earth.[5]

Logsdon points to another passage of Scripture that mentions Babylon, Jeremiah 50–51, to identify sixteen parallels between Babylon and modern America. His conclusion: America will be destroyed in the last days by a great alliance of nations from the north, probably led by Russia, that will use devastating weapons to strike unexpectedly, suddenly, and decisively.[6]

Jack Van Impe, a popular television prophecy teacher, also points to Jeremiah 50–51 and Revelation 18 as describing America in the last days. In his book *The Great Escape,* he points out several similarities between Babylon and the United States. Then he concludes, "That, my friends, is a graphic picture of the United States of America."[7]

In another of his books, Van Impe says this:

In Revelation, chapter 18, John the Apostle also alludes to this nation—a rich land laden with sins that has glorified herself and lived deliciously.

As I continue to read and study the prophetic writings of Scripture, I become more and more convinced that this is a direct reference to the United States. The present hedonistic pleasure-craze of our nation will not last forever. America's destruction may come quick as lightning.[8]

AMERICA, THE BABYLON?

The most extensive, in-depth treatment of the view that America is the Babylon of the last days comes from author R. A. Coombes in his book *America, the Babylon: America's Destiny Foretold in Biblical Prophecy*.

Coombes closely examines Jeremiah 50–51 and several chapters from Isaiah (see 13–14; 18; 21; 24; 47–48). Then he identifies thirty-three markers that he says show that Babylon in the last days is the leading city in America: New York City. Here are ten of his more interesting points:

1. Future Babylon will be the last of the superpowers (see Jeremiah 50:12).
2. Future Babylon is where a body of the world's leaders assembles and meets (see Jeremiah 51:44).

3. Future Babylon is the world's policeman (see Jeremiah 50:23).

4. Future Babylon is extremely wealthy (see Jeremiah 51:13).

5. Future Babylon is a land of immigrants (see Jeremiah 50:16).

6. Future Babylon has no fear of invasion on its home soil (see Isaiah 47:5, 8).

7. Future Babylon is noted for its disrespect of the elderly (see Isaiah 47:6).

8. Future Babylon is a military air power and a land of air travel; it would seem to have massive air power capability (see Isaiah 18:1).

9. Future Babylon is seemingly connected to outer space (just as ancient Babylon was with its tower of Babel), and that connection is perhaps more than simply observing the stars (see Jeremiah 51:53).

10. Future Babylon seems to have something akin to stealth technology (see Isaiah 47:10–13).[9]

Then Coombes turns to the Babylon of Revelation 17–18. He presents a sixty-six-point list that identifies it with New York City. Once again, here are ten of his more interesting points:

1. New York City is the location of the only world-governing body, the United Nations (see Revelation 17:2, 8).

2. New York City is the city of commerce; these commodities trade daily:
   • coffee, sugar, and cocoa—traded at the Coffee, Sugar, and Cocoa Exchange;
   • cotton and orange juice—traded at the New York Cotton Exchange;
   • crude oil, gasoline, natural gas, heating oil, platinum, and palladium—traded at the New York Mercantile Exchange;
   • gold, silver, and copper—traded at the New York Mercantile Comex Division (see Revelation 18:11–13);
   • diamonds, precious gems, iron, ivory, marble, spices, cosmetics, legal pharmaceutical drugs, and professional services especially related to advertising, media, and the arts;

    • fine foreign wines from around the world (see Revelation 18:11–13).

3. New York City is home to:
   • the New York Stock Exchange;
   • the American Stock Exchange;
   • NASDAQ;
   • the biggest banks, including the Federal Reserve Bank, the biggest in the world; it is the "engine of wealth" for the world economy (see Revelation 18:15, 19).

4. New York City is a deep-water port city, one of the world's greatest seaports ever (see Revelation 18:17–19).

5. New York City is the key cultural city of the world (see Revelation 18:22).

6. New York City is the largest consumer of illicit drugs, especially heavy drugs like heroin and cocaine (see Revelation 18:23).

7. New York City is and always has been a city of immigrants (see Revelation 18:15).

8. New York City is the place for merchandising occultism (see Revelation 18:23).

9. New York City has the largest population of Jews in America; further, the U.S. is home to more Jewish people than anywhere in the world, including Israel. New York City and the U.S. share this distinction with ancient Babylon (see Revelation 18:4; Jeremiah 50:8, 28; 51:6, 45–46).

10. On Long Island, overlooking one of the main harbor approaches to New York City and within view of the Statue of Liberty, is the community of Babylon, New York. This community received its name because of the large influx of Jewish immigrants settling in the area; the Jewish population began to grow reminiscent of the Jewish exiles from ancient Babylon.[10]

Another key point that Coombes focuses on is the alleged similarity between the Statue of Liberty and the woman riding the beast in Revelation 17–18. He notes the following parallels:

THE WOMAN ON THE BEAST	STATUE OF LIBERTY
Robed in scarlet or purple	Robed (originally in scarlet/purple)
Golden cup in her hand	Originally a golden cup, changed to a torch
Purple robes denotes royalty; we can imagine her wearing a crown	Crown of seven spikes or horns
Cup contents: smelly pollutants connected to immigrants (see Revelation 17:15)	Cup contents: natural gas flame connected to immigrants
She sits on seven heads— mountains or continents	The seven spikes or horns on her crown represents the seven continents
Represents Babylon the megacity	Overlooks Babylon on Long Island; supposed to be a representation of the goddess "Liberty," aka Aphrodite, Venus, Isis, and ultimately Ishtar—the primary goddess of Babylon
Reigns over the kings of the earth	Overlooks the UN building
Mother of harlots	Mother of exiles, according to the poem on the base of the statue.[11]

OBJECTION, YOUR HONOR!

I believe that neither America nor New York City is the Babylon of Revelation 17–18. For one thing, Babylon is presented as a wicked *city* (not a nation) that persecutes God's people, especially the prophets and saints (see Revelation 17:6; 18:24). Though we may agree that New York City has a great deal of wickedness, as do all big cities, it has consistently been a safe haven to which Jews and Christians from all over the world have been able to flee in order to escape persecution.

Another reason I don't think Babylon is America or New York City is that a better theory is out there, a theory that does the best job of identifying the Babylon of Revelation.

I believe that Revelation 17–18 is referring to *a literal, rebuilt city of Babylon* in modern-day Iraq. At the end of the Tribulation, God will visit this city on the Euphrates River and destroy it. There are seven reasons why I think this theory is best.

First, six times in Revelation, the great city that is described as the last-days capital of Antichrist is specifically called *Babylon* (see 14:8; 16:19; 17:5; 18:2, 10, 21). While it is possible that the name *Babylon* is a code name for Rome, New York City, Jerusalem, or some other city, nothing in the text indicates that it is to be taken figuratively or symbolically. Therefore, it is best to take it as a reference to literal Babylon.

The second reason I think Revelation indicates that Babylon is a literal city is that the Bible mentions the city more times than any other city except Jerusalem: about 290 times. Whenever it is mentioned in Scripture, Babylon is pictured as the epitome of evil and rebellion against God. Babylon is Satan's capital city on earth.

- Babylon is the city where man first began to worship himself in an organized rebellion against God (see Genesis 11:1–9).
- Babylon was the capital city of the first world ruler, Nimrod (see Genesis 10:8–10; 11:9).
- Nebuchadnezzar, king of Babylon, destroyed the city of Jerusalem and the temple in 586 B.C.
- Babylon was the capital city of the first of four Gentile world empires to rule over Jerusalem.

Since Babylon was the capital city of the first world ruler and is pictured as Satan's capital city on earth throughout Scripture, it makes sense that in the end times he will once again raise up this city as the capital city of the final world ruler.

In Charles Dyer's excellent book *The Rise of Babylon,* he says this:

> Throughout history, Babylon has represented the height of rebellion and opposition to God's plans and purposes, so God allows Babylon to continue during the final days. It is almost as though he "calls her out" for a final duel. But this time, the conflict between God and Babylon ends decisively. The city of Babylon will be destroyed.[12]

A third argument in favor of Babylon's being a literal city is that a rebuilt Babylon would fit the criteria laid out in Revelation 17–18. As respected New Testament scholar Robert Thomas notes:

> Babylon on the Euphrates has a location that fits this description politically, geographically, and in all the qualities of accessibility, commercial

facilities, remoteness of interferences of church and state, and yet centrality in regard to the trade of the whole world.[13]

Fourth, the Euphrates River is mentioned by name twice in Revelation (see 9:14; 16:12). In the first passage, the text states that four fallen angels are being held at the Euphrates River, awaiting the appointed time for them to lead forth a host of demons to destroy one-third of mankind. In Revelation 16:12, the sixth bowl judgment is poured out and dries up the Euphrates River to prepare the way for the kings of the east.

These references to the Euphrates River—a literal, geographic place—point to the fact that something important and evil is occurring there. The rebuilt city of Babylon on the Euphrates, functioning as a religious and political center for Antichrist, is a good explanation for this emphasis on the Euphrates River in Revelation.

The fifth argument to support the idea that the Babylon of Revelation is a rebuilt city in Iraq is the incredible vision recorded in Zechariah 5:5–11.

Notice that this is referring to a literal city of Babylon in the last days.

> Then the angel who was talking with me came forward and said, "Look up! Something is appearing in the sky."
>
> "What is it?" I asked.
>
> He replied, "It is a basket for measuring grain, and it is filled with the sins of everyone throughout the land."
>
> When the heavy lead cover was lifted off the basket, there was a woman sitting inside it. The angel said, "The woman's name is Wickedness," and he pushed her back into the basket and closed the heavy lid again.
>
> Then I looked up and saw two women flying toward us, with wings gliding on the wind. Their wings were like those of a stork, and they picked up the basket and flew with it into the sky.
>
> "Where are they taking the basket?" I asked the angel.
>
> He replied, "To the land of Babylonia, where they will build a temple for the basket.

And when the temple is ready, they will set the basket there on its pedestal." (NLT)

The prophet Zechariah was writing in about 520 B.C., twenty years after the fall of Babylon to the Medo-Persians. He saw evil returning to its original place in

ZECHARIAH 5:5–11	REVELATION 17–18
Woman sitting in a basket	Woman sitting on the beast, seven mountains, and many waters
Emphasis on commerce (a basket for measuring grain)	Emphasis on commerce (merchant of grain)
Woman's name is Wickedness	Woman's name is "Babylon the Great, Mother of All Prostitutes and Obscenities in the world"
Focus on false worship (a temple is built for the woman)	Focus on false worship
Woman is taken to Babylon	Woman is called Babylon

the future. In this vision, Zechariah sees a woman who is named Wickedness. Then he sees this woman carried away in a basket during the last days to the land of Babylonia, where a temple will be built for her.

The parallels between Zechariah 5:5–11 and Revelation 17–18 are striking:

Here God's Word seems to be teaching that in the end times, wickedness will again rear its ugly head in the same place where it began—Babylon. The prostitute written about by the apostle John will fulfill Zechariah 5, and in the last days, Babylon will once again be established as the city that embodies evil.

Sixth, Isaiah 13 and Jeremiah 50–51 predict that the city of Babylon will be suddenly and completely destroyed. Since this has never happened, it is reasonable to conclude that these Scriptures refer to a future city of Babylon that will be totally destroyed in the Tribulation.

The seventh and final reason I believe that Revelation's Babylon is a rebuilt Babylon in Iraq is that Jeremiah 50–51 clearly describe the geographical city of Babylon on the Euphrates. The many parallels between this passage and the future Babylon in

Revelation 17–18 (see the table on the following page) indicate that they are both describing the same city.[14]

PARALLELS BETWEEN JEREMIAH 50–51 AND REVELATION 17–18		
Description of Babylon	**Jeremiah 50–51**	**Revelation 17–18**
Compared to a golden cup	51:7a	17:3–4; 18:6
Dwelling on many waters	51:13a	17:7
Involved with nations	51:7b	17:2
Named the same	50:1	18:10
Destroyed suddenly	51:8a	18:8
Destroyed by fire	51:30b	17:16
Never to be inhabited	50:39	18:21
Punished according to her works	50:29	18:6
Fall illustrated	51:63–64	18:21
God's people flee	51:6, 45	18:4
Heaven to rejoice	51:48	18:20

CONCLUSION

Because of these seven reasons, I believe that Babylon in Revelation 17–18 is *not* New York City or America. Instead, I believe that the ancient city of Babylon will be rebuilt in Iraq in the last days to serve as the religious and commercial capital for the Antichrist's empire. Wickedness will return to this place for its final stand. Then, in the seventh bowl judgment at the end of the Tribulation, God will put it in Antichrist's heart to destroy the great city of Babylon with fire (see Revelation 17:16–17; 18:8). Finally, Babylon will fall, never to rise again!

The rise of Iraq in recent years on the world political and economic scene is not an accident. There is a divine reason that she possesses huge reservoirs of oil—and receives great profits from it. In spite of the Gulf War and tremendous worldwide pressure, Iraq remains a formidable foe. This current rebuilding and rise of Babylon may be a key part of God's plan for the last days.

Revelation 17–18 is the first of three passages that people often point to as referring to America in the end times. Now that we have found that this passage doesn't allude to America, we can move on to another passage as we continue to ask the question, Is America in Bible Prophecy?

THREE

IS AMERICA THE UNNAMED NATION IN ISAIAH 18?

In the quest to find America in the pages of Scripture, another passage that is commonly cited as a reference to the United States is Isaiah 18. This interesting chapter refers to a great nation (not specifically identified by name) whose people are fierce and enterprising. In the first two verses of the chapter, Isaiah issues a warning to this nation:

> Woe to the land shadowing with wings, which is beyond the rivers of Ethiopia: That sendeth ambassadors by the sea, even in vessels

of bulrushes upon the waters, saying, Go, ye swift messengers, to a nation scattered and peeled, to a people terrible from their beginning hitherto; a nation meted out and trodden down, whose land the rivers have spoiled! (v v. 1–2, KJV)

In his book *The Great Escape,* Jack Van Impe supports the view that this is a reference to America.

Isaiah 18:1–2 issues a warning to a nation.... The nation described in this text is in great difficulty with God because the opening word "woe" in the text is judgmental. The nation has the insignia of wings, similar to America's national emblem, the bald eagle. It is a land that is beyond the sea from Israel. This designation of "beyond Ethiopia" eliminates all of the nations of Europe, Asia and Africa. It is a land scattered and peeled, meaning it is stretched out and having a large landmass. It is measured and staked out with counties, cities, and states. It is a land with polluted rivers.

Does that not sound unmistakably like our precious America?[15]

The phrase "whose land the rivers have spoiled" is better translated "whose land the rivers divide." Some see this as a clear reference to America since America is divided east and west from Canada to the Gulf of Mexico by the Mississippi River and is further divided by the Ohio, Tennessee, Missouri, Arkansas, and Columbia Rivers.[16]

THE KINGDOM OF CUSH

In spite of these creative attempts to link America to Isaiah 18, the overwhelming biblical evidence comes down *against* identifying America with the nation mentioned in Isaiah 18.

Isaiah 18 fits into a longer section, chapters 18–20, that is one connected prophecy dealing with the ancient nations of Cush and Egypt, which were one country at that time. Ancient Cush included modern-day southern Egypt, Sudan, northern Ethiopia, and Somalia. The phrase "the land shadowing with wings" does not refer to the wings of an eagle, but the whirring wings of insects that infested the Nile valley in that area.[17]

In Isaiah 18:1–2, God is warning the Cushites to get in their boats and head back home and not form an alliance against the Assyrians. God promises that when it was time for the Assyrians to fall, He Himself would destroy them for all the surrounding nations to see: "All you inhabitants of the world and dwellers on earth, as soon as a standard is raised on the mountains, you will see it, and as soon as the trumpet is blown, you will hear it" (Isaiah 18:3).

I will conclude this short chapter by saying this: If we want to find America in Bible prophecy, we will have to look somewhere besides Isaiah 18.

Now let's check out the third biblical passage often said to refer to America in the last days.

IS AMERICA "THE YOUNG LIONS OF TARSHISH"?

nother Scripture that has often been cited as a reference to the United States is Ezekiel 38:13:

"Sheba and Dedan and the merchants of Tarshish with all its villages will say to you, 'Have you come to capture spoil? Have you assembled your company to seize plunder, to carry away silver and gold, to take away cattle and goods, to capture great spoil?'"

In order for us to understand Ezekiel 38:13, we need to understand a little background from the overall setting of Ezekiel 38–39. These two chapters, written over twenty-five hundred years ago, predict a last-days invasion of the land of Israel by a massive attack force. The invaders will be led by a man called "Gog" who will be the final ruler of Russia (or "Rosh").

Ezekiel 38:1–6 provides a compelling list of the specific nations that will invade Israel in the end times.

RUSSIA'S ALLIES IN THE BATTLE OF GOG AND MAGOG	
Ancient Nation	**Modern Nation**
Magog (ancient Scythians)	Central Asia (Kazakhstan, Tajikistan, Turkmenistan, Kyrgyzstan, Uzbekistan, and possibly Afghanistan)
Meshech	Turkey
Tubal	Turkey
Persia	Iran
Ethiopia (Cush)	Sudan
Libya (Put)	Libya
Gomer	Turkey
Beth-togarmah	Turkey

As you can see from this list, several key nations will come against Israel in the end times: Russia, Iran, Sudan, Libya, Turkey, and at least some if not all of the nations of Central Asia.

It's also quite interesting in light of our world political climate today to note that all of these nations (except Russia) are Muslim nations. And many of these hate the nation of Israel and would jump at the opportunity to wipe her off the face of the earth.

TRACKING THE BEAR

In late 1991 and early 1992 when the Soviet Union came tumbling down, many people thought that Russia was a modern-day Humpty Dumpty—finished. The consensus seemed to be that the Russian bear had gone into permanent hibernation. But this may not be so.

The Bible predicts that a great northern nation named "Rosh" will, with many allies, invade Israel in the end times. I believe that Rosh is a reference to the nation we know today as Russia.

At the time Ezekiel was writing his prophecy, a certain group of people lived to the north of Israel.

They were variously known as the Rus, Ros, Rashu, and Rasapu. In 200 B.C. this fierce people poured into the southern part of what we know today as Russia. The great Hebrew scholar Wilhelm Gesenius wrote that Rosh is "a northern nation...undoubtedly the Russians...dwelling to the north of Taurus...on the river *Rha* (Wolga)."[18]

When we track Russia and her allies listed in Ezekiel 38, we soon discover that the trail leads right into the land of Israel:

> "You will come from your place out of the remote parts of the north, you and many peoples with you, all of them riding on horses, a great assembly and a mighty army; and you will come up against My people Israel like a cloud to cover the land." (vv. 15–16a)

WHEN GOG MEETS GOD

When Russia and her allies come sweeping into the land of Israel, God will wipe them out. Ezekiel describes the Lord's fearsome wrath against Gog and his army:

"It will come about on that day, when Gog comes against the land of Israel," declares the Lord GOD, "that My fury will mount up in My anger. In My zeal and in My blazing wrath I declare that on that day there will surely be a great earthquake in the land of Israel. The fish of the sea, the birds of the heavens, the beasts of the field, all the creeping things that creep on the earth, and all the men who are on the face of the earth will shake at My presence; the mountains also will be thrown down, the steep pathways will collapse and every wall will fall to the ground. I will call for a sword against him on all My mountains," declares the Lord GOD. "Every man's sword will be against his brother. With pestilence and with blood I will enter into judgment with him; and I will rain on him and on his troops, and on the many peoples who are with him, a torrential rain, with hailstones, fire and brimstone." (Ezekiel 38:18–22)

God will utterly destroy Gog and his allies by earthquake, infighting among the troops, pestilence (disease), and fire from heaven.

This invasion of Israel will probably occur some-time just before the middle of the seven-year Tribulation. The annihilation of Russia's army and the vast majority of the military power of the Arab/Muslim world just before the midpoint of the Tribulation will pave the way for Antichrist to invade Israel himself and establish his three-and-a-half-year world empire.

ANTIWAR PROTESTERS

You might be wondering at this point what all this has to do with America in the last days? Let me show you the connection that many prophecy scholars see.

Ezekiel 38:13 says that when Russia and her last-days allies descend upon the land of Israel, a small group of nations will lamely protest the invasion:

> "Sheba and Dedan and the merchants of Tarshish with all its villages will say to you, 'Have you come to capture spoil? Have you assembled your company to seize plunder, to carry away silver and gold, to take away cattle and goods, to capture great spoil?'"

The specific nations that question Gog's actions are identified as "Sheba and Dedan and the merchants of Tarshish." Sheba and Dedan are not difficult to identify. These are the ancient names for the land we know today as Saudi Arabia.

Tarshish, on the other hand, is not so simple to identify. But the majority of scholars believe that Tarshish is ancient Tartessus in the present-day nation of Spain. Both Brown-Driver-Briggs and the Hebrew scholar Gesenius support this view. Tarshish was a wealthy, flourishing colony of the Phoenicians. It exported silver, iron, tin, and lead (see Jeremiah 10:9; Ezekiel 27:12, 25).

But note that Ezekiel refers not only to Tarshish, but also to "the merchants of Tarshish with all its villages." The better translation is probably "Tarshish, with all the young lions" (KJV). The New International Version cites "her strong lions" as an alternate reading.

Young lions are often used in Scripture to refer to energetic rulers. Therefore, the young lions who act with Tarshish to verbally oppose Gog's invasion may be strong military and political leaders who act in concert with Tarshish.

Where was Tarshish in Ezekiel's day? It was at the extreme west of the known world, in Spain. When God commanded Jonah to go preach to Nineveh (about five hundred miles northeast of Israel), Jonah headed to Tarshish instead—about as far in the other direction as he could go (see Jonah 1:1–3).

Tarshish is associated in Scripture with the West: "The western kings of Tarshish and the islands will bring him tribute" (Psalm 72:10, NLT). Therefore, Ezekiel may have been using Tarshish as a way of representing the nations of Western Europe who will join Saudi Arabia in denouncing the Russian-led invasion of Israel.

The young lions of Tarshish could be a reference to the colonies that emerged from Europe—including the United States. If this is true, then the young lions of Tarshish could be the United States in the last days. If so, she will join with her European and Saudi allies to lodge a formal protest against the Russian-Islamic aggressors.

Several well-known prophecy teachers favor this view. Ed Hindson says, "As a nation of European transplants, the United States could possibly qualify as the 'young lions' of Tarshish."[19] Jack Van Impe also believes that America is one of the young lions of Tarshish:

> It's true that America is not mentioned in the Bible by name. However, it is written that "all nations" will suffer judgment in the days before the return of our Lord Jesus Christ (Micah 5:15; Ezekiel 39:2). Ezekiel 38:13 does single out Tarshish and all her "young lions," a group of nations that pays a heavy price for coming to the defense of Israel when it is invaded by Russia and a coalition of other nations. The name Tarshish is found twenty times in the Bible and always refers to the land farthest west of Israel. The text refers to the eleven merchants of Tarshish, and explains that these people trade goods around the world. Specifically, I believe Tarshish refers to Britain, and all her "young lions" refers to the English-speaking world—including the United States.[20]

David Allen Lewis also supports this view:

Conservative scholars who interpret the Ezekiel passage literally have tended to identify Tarshish as Great Britain. The young lions thereof would be the English-speaking nations of the world such as the U.S. and Canada.... This leads us to the exciting conclusion—that this is the one prophecy of the Bible that can be identified with the U.S.... So the young lions of Tarshish would definitely refer to the North American colonies as well as the European colonies, and hence bring the U.S. into this prophecy as one of the nations who will strongly protest the Russian invasion of Israel in the last days.[21]

Although I do not believe that the young lions of Tarshish are a reference to the United States, I concede that of all the passages in the Bible that *could* refer to the United States, this is by far the best one.

THE CURRENT ALIGNMENT
OF NATIONS

Whether you take these young lions as a reference to the United States or as just a reference to the Western powers of the last days, the scenario that is developed in Ezekiel 38 fits the present world political situation precisely.

Russia continues to build alliances with Middle Eastern nations. Sudan (Cush) and Iran (Persia) are strong allies. The Muslim nations of Central Asia (Magog) have developing ties with Iran, Russia, and Turkey. The hatred for Israel by the Middle Eastern Muslim nations continues to boil. It is not too difficult to imagine the nations mentioned in Ezekiel 38:1–6 coming together under Russian leadership to mount a furious attack against Israel.

But what is the one Middle East nation that consistently sides with the West against the radical Islamic elements in that region of the world? The obvious answer is Saudi Arabia—ancient Sheba and Dedan. As one illustration of this alliance, consider that the U.S. and NATO use bases in Saudi Arabia to launch strikes against Iraq and to monitor the entire Persian Gulf area.

The exact alignment of nations predicted in Ezekiel 38 was clearly evidenced in the Gulf War. The United States, Western Europe, and Saudi Arabia were allied against Iraq, while Russia, Iran, Sudan, Libya and most of the other nations of the Middle East and Persian Gulf were aligned with Iraq or at least against America. To a large degree that alignment remains in effect today.

CONCLUSION

Let's pause here for a brief review of the ground we've covered thus far. Remember, we have rejected the idea that the United States or New York City is Babylon because neither fits the description of Babylon in Revelation 17–18. These two chapters fit much better if we link them with the literal city of Babylon in modern Iraq.

We've also rejected the view that America is the unnamed nation in Isaiah 18, because that chapter is a clear historical reference to ancient Cush in Africa. Finally, we've concluded that the reference to the young lions of Tarshish in Ezekiel 38 probably alludes to Western Europe, not the United States.

Therefore, I conclude that the role of the United States in the end times is *not* specifically discussed in the Bible.

This is actually quite remarkable when you think about it. If we are living in the latter years of this age, doesn't it seem logical that God would clarify the role of the most powerful, influential nation in the history of the world? But He didn't. Why not?

Over the years prophecy scholars have struggled to answer this question. In the next chapter we will turn to four possible explanations for why the United States is not mentioned in Bible prophecy.

FIVE

THE SOUNDS OF SILENCE

As much as we desire to know about America's future from Bible prophecy, we have to face the fact that our nation is not clearly referred to. Noted prophecy expert Tim LaHaye observes: "One of the hardest things for American prophecy students to accept is that the United States is not clearly mentioned in Bible prophecy, yet our nation is the only superpower in the world today."[22]

It would be nice if Scripture clearly laid out the role of the United States in the last days, but the silence of Scripture on this subject may tell us more than we realize. The sounds of silence may actually provide us with the crucial clue concerning the place of America in the last days.

THE FUTURE OF
THE UNITED STATES

If America is not specifically referred to in any Bible prophecies, how should we interpret this scriptural silence? I cannot speak with certainty at this point, but I can make some educated guesses. I believe we can choose from four basic options.

Option 1 is that America will still be a powerful nation in the last days, but the Lord simply chose not to mention her specifically.

This is possible, but it seems unlikely. In Scripture, the dominant political and military power in the end times is centered in the Mediterranean and in Europe. The scriptural silence concerning America seems to indicate that by the time the tribulation period arrives, America will no longer be a major influence in the world.

John Walvoord, one of the foremost experts in Bible prophecy, agrees:

Although conclusions concerning the role of America in prophecy in the end time are necessarily tentative, the Scriptural evidence is sufficient to conclude that America in that day will not be a major power and apparently does not figure largely in either the political, economic, or religious aspects of the world.[23]

Of course, this raises another very important question: How can this be? America is the major player in the world today in every arena; what will happen to reduce her to a subordinate role in world affairs? If the scriptural silence indicates that America will be a relatively unimportant nation in the end times, how will America fall?

The other three options address this issue.

Option 2 is that America is not mentioned specifically in Scripture because she will be destroyed by other nations. She will suffer a fall from the outside.

Those who hold to this theory are quick to point to the notion that America will be crippled by a nuclear attack. However, in recent days the terrorist attacks on our nation have led some to conclude that our own freedom and technology will be the Achilles' heel that brings us down.

Option 3 is that America is not mentioned in Bible prophecy because she will have lost her influence as a result of moral and spiritual deterioration. She will suffer a fall from the inside.

As you can imagine, this is a very popular view today in light of the moral malaise we see all around us. Proponents of this view have no trouble citing alarming statistics related to drug use, alcoholism, teen pregnancy, children born out of wedlock, divorce, pornography, abortion, homosexuality, and on and on.

Option 4 is the subject of the next chapter. Any of these first three options is certainly possible, but there is a fourth option that I believe best explains the silence concerning America in the Scriptures.

I think you will find it quite interesting.

THE LATE GREAT UNITED STATES

If America will not fall from *within* due to her moral corruption or from without by nuclear attack or terrorism, how do we explain the fact that America seems to be such a second-rate nation in the last days that it does not even warrant specific mention in the Bible?

As John Walvoord admits, "Any final answer to the question is therefore an impossibility, but nevertheless some conclusions of a general character can be reached."[24] Let me share with you the three main points of reasoning that lead me to "some conclusions of a general character."

FRIENDS OF ISRAEL

First, America today is the number one ally and defender of Israel. Our economic and military aid to Israel each year totals somewhere in the neighborhood of $3–4 billion, depending on which statistics you use.

According to the Congressional Research Service, from 1949–2000 the United States has given Israel a total of $81.38 billion in aid. Others place the total as high as $91 billion. Roughly 20 percent of American foreign aid money goes to Israel. American aid makes up 7 to 8 percent of the total Israeli national budget. Militarily, too, the situation is clear: Without the support of the United States, Israel would be incinerated in a matter of days by her hostile Arab neighbors.

But Israel is pictured in Scripture as a thriving nation in the end times. Therefore, unless the world scene changes dramatically, I believe that America will remain strong as a nation until the beginning of the end times. Until the Rapture, the United States will continue to serve as Israel's chief ally.

ANTICHRIST STEPS IN

Second, we know from Scripture that after the Rapture, the Antichrist will come to Israel's side and make a seven-year treaty with her (see Daniel 9:27). But where is America in that scenario? Why aren't we around as Israel's great protector?

Evidently, Antichrist and his European empire will replace America as Israel's chief ally and as the major world power (see Daniel 2:44–45; 7:23–25). This strong presence of Europe indicates to me that something will have happened to America that shifts world power back to Europe.

THE RAPTURE FACTOR

Third, if America remains strong up to the time of the Rapture but is then replaced by Europe as the world's superpower, what does this tell us?

I believe it tells us that America will be brought to her knees by the Rapture. The Rapture is the key. The Rapture will change everything. There's an old saying: "Nature abhors a vacuum." I believe the Rapture will produce a power vacuum—and into it will step the Antichrist and his reunited Roman Empire.

Think about it. If the Rapture were to happen today and all the true believers in Jesus Christ were whisked away to heaven in a split second, America would be devastated. Consider these most recent statistics from Barna Research Online:

- 85 percent of Americans claim to be "Christians." This group is often identified as "cultural Christians."
- 41 percent of Americans claim to be "born-again Christians"; this is a subset of the broad "Christian" group.
- 8 percent of American adults identify themselves as "evangelical Christians." This group is a subset of the "born-again" group; the main factor in this category is a belief that salvation is by faith in Christ alone, without human works. According to Barna, this represents about 15 to 20 million American adults; adding in children, the number could easily climb to 25 to 30 million.[25]

In his book *Operation World*, Patrick Johnstone

records the number of evangelical Christians in America as 23 percent of the total population. The 2000 census found that the total population of America is 281,421,906. Using Johnstone's percentage, the total number of believers in America is about 65 million.[26]

So at the Rapture, America will lose somewhere between 25 and 65 million citizens: Christians and their small children.[27] The impact of such a disappearance will be nothing short of cataclysmic. Not only would our country lose a minimum of 10 percent of her population, but she would also lose the very best, the "salt and light" of this great land (see Matthew 5:13–14).

The same cannot be legitimately said of any other nation in the world. Patrick Johnstone gives the following statistics for the number of evangelicals in various regions of the world:[28]

United States	23 percent
Africa	11.4 percent
Latin America	9.1 percent
Asia	2.7 percent
Middle East	.3 percent

The numbers for Europe are staggering. The new Europe includes forty-five states with a total population in excess of half a billion people. Yet twenty-two of these states have less than 1 percent evangelical Christians. Overall, Europe is less than 2 percent evangelical Christian.[29]

The reality of how few believers are in other parts of the world really hit home back in 1998 when I was on a study trip to Turkey.

One night I was on a bus traveling from Ephesus to Izmir, a city of about 3 million people. When we neared Izmir, I got a glimpse of the city shimmering in the night. As I looked from the bus and surveyed the massive city, I realized that if the Rapture were to occur right now, these poor people would never know the difference. Only about two hundred Christians live in Izmir, according to a Turkish pastor who lives there. Two hundred people out of 3 million would hardly be missed.

To many nations and whole regions of the world, the Rapture will be nothing more than a blip on the radar screen.

But not so in America. The ripple effect of the Rapture will touch every area of our society. Millions of mortgages will go unpaid, military personnel by the thousands will be permanently AWOL, factory workers will never again show up for work, college tuitions will become overdue, businesses will be left without workers and leaders, the Dow will crash, the NAS-DAQ will plummet, and the entire economy will be thrown into chaos.

Charles Dyer describes the impact of the Rapture on America:

> Today as many as half of all Americans claim to be "born again," or believers in Jesus Christ. If only one-fourth of that number have genuinely made a personal commitment to Christ, then over 28 million Americans will suddenly "disappear" when God removes his church from the earth.
>
> Can you imagine the effects on our country if over 28 million people—people in industry, government, the military, business, agriculture, education, medicine and communications—disappear? That is approximately double the entire population of New York

City, Los Angeles, Chicago, and Houston all rolled together!

The economic fluctuations of the eighties and even the Great Depression will pale in comparison to the political and economic collapse that will occur when our society suddenly loses individuals who were its "salt and light." America could not support an army in the Middle East because the military would be needed at home to control the chaos![30]

The Rapture may well be the end of America as we know it. Those who miss out on the Rapture in the United States will be left behind to pick up the pieces.

SELAH

In Hebrew, the word *selah* means to pause—to stop, look, and listen. With all the ground we've covered, this would be a great place to pull over and park for a moment to see where we are.

Here are the seven conclusions we have reached up to this point:

1. America is not mentioned in the Bible.
2. America is currently Israel's main ally and defender.
3. America must remain strong until the end times to continue her defense of Israel.
4. The scriptural silence concerning America in the end times seems to indicate that America will fall from her position of world prominence.
5. World power in the end times will be centered in the reunited Roman Empire (Europe).
6. European prominence can be explained only in light of a decline in power of America. Why else would Europe guarantee Israel's safety unless something had happened to the United States?
7. America will fall when the church is raptured.

ONE MORE PIECE TO THE PUZZLE

But this raises a new question: After the decline she suffers at the Rapture, what will America do? What will become of her after her fall? What will a postrapture America look like?

In the next chapter we will look at a probable scenario of the last days of the United States of America.

SEVEN

AMERICA IN THE LAST DAYS

S ince America is not mentioned or referred to specifically in any passage of Scripture, we must be careful about drawing any hard and fast conclusions about her future. Nothing on this subject can be stated with certainty. However, in my studies I have discovered a fairly broad consensus among prophecy scholars concerning the destiny of the United States.

Simply stated, the main view is that in the end times, America will be absorbed into Antichrist's reunited Roman Empire. The United States will become a part of the end-time confederacy of Western nations.

This conclusion is reached primarily by looking at two key clues, one from our past and one from our present.

A Hint from Our Heritage

The first clue concerning the future of America is derived from looking at our origins as a nation. Since America began as a European colony, it seems reasonable that after the Rapture, America will return to her European roots to find stability amid the chaos.

Charles Ryrie looks to America's European origins as a key to her future in the end times:

It is not too far-fetched to envision the United States someday aligned with the Western Confederation of Nations which will be formed by Antichrist. National origin could be the link, since many United States citizens originally came from the countries which will make up that Western alliance of nations.... So when the European Federation of Nations rises to power, the United States may find herself in a supportive role in favor of this powerful alliance and in opposition to the other power blocs in Russia, Africa, and the Far East. This would mean that the United States, haven for Christianity for two centuries, will find herself in league with Antichrist.[31]

"Go West, Young Man"

The other main clue concerning America's future comes from her current status as not only a superpower, but also a Western superpower. America is a Western nation in every way.

During the Tribulation, Scripture indicates that the world will be divided into four main power blocs led by four sovereigns.

1. *The King of the North* (see Daniel 11:40)—I believe that this is a northern coalition of nations led by Russia. In Daniel 11:5–35, the historical king of the north was the leader of the Seleucid empire. This was centered in Syria but included a vast territory north and east of Israel. The prophetic counterpart to the Seleucid "king of the north" seems to be the

great northern confederacy headed by Russia (see also Ezekiel 38–39).

2. *The King of the South* (see Daniel 11:40)—This appears to be the leader of Egypt who directs a Muslim league of nations.

3. *The Kings of the East* (see Revelation 16:12)— All we know about these nations is that they come from east of the Euphrates River to gather at Armageddon for the final great conflict of this age. The kings of the east could include modern Afghanistan, India, Pakistan, China, Japan, and/or Korea.

4. *The King of the West* (see Daniel 2:40–43)— Although the Antichrist is never actually called the "king of the west," as the leader of the reunited Roman Empire centered in Europe this is an apt title for him. This king will lead the confederation of Western nations during the final three and a half years of the Tribulation and will ultimately expand his empire to include the entire world (see Revelation 13:4–8).

Not every nation is mentioned in end-times prophecy, but these are the four great confederations that will be present in the end times. It appears that most of the nations of the world will be allied with one of these power blocs at one time or another.

Which of these power blocs would the United States probably join when the nations of the earth scramble for position and build alliances after the Rapture? Where would we naturally gravitate? The Western alliance, of course. Why? Because that's who we are strongly tied to today. Through NATO we are bound to the nations of Western Europe.

Ed Dobson, a well-known pastor and prophecy teacher, says this:

> But we know that when the Eastern coalition armies begin their invasion of Israel for the Battle of Armageddon, they will be opposed by the Antichrist and a coalition of Western nations (Revelation 16:12–14). The United States will most likely be part of that coalition because it is a Western superpower.[32]

John Walvoord also sees the United States in league with Europe in the end times:

> Although the Scriptures do not give any clear word concerning the role of the Unites States in relationship to the revived Roman Empire and the later development of the world empire, it is probable that the United States will be in some form of alliance with the Roman ruler. Most citizens of the United States of America have come from Europe and their sympathies would be more naturally with a European alliance than with Russia or countries in Eastern Asia.... Based on geographic, religious and economic factors, such an alliance of powers seems a natural sequence of present situations in the world.[33]

AMERICA R.I.P.

The amalgamation of America into the Antichrist's European empire after the Rapture doesn't seem nearly as far-fetched as it used to. In fact, it makes perfect sense in the current political climate.

The United States is slowly, subtly, but relentlessly being drawn away from national sovereignty into globalism. NATO, the UN, GATT, NAFTA, WTO, and many other acronyms signal the startling trend away from U.S. sovereignty toward submission to multinational treaties, organizations, and courts of law.

When the trumpet sounds and all the Christians in the United States disappear, the final countdown to the end of America's sovereignty will begin. Before she knows it, America will find herself taking her place in the kingdom of Antichrist.

I know it hurts true American patriots like you and me to think that America could fall—or even worse, that the land we love could end up in league with the Antichrist—but I believe that that is what the Bible implies. What a sad ending for a nation that was originally founded as "one nation under God."

Does this mean we should throw in the towel? Should we give up on America and move somewhere else? God forbid! As long as the Lord gives us breath, we should continue to do all we can for the spiritual well-being of our nation and our world. After all, we don't know how long it may be until the Lord comes.

In the next chapter let's consider what we can do to secure the continued blessing of God upon our great nation.

GOD BLESS AMERICA!

In the past few months I have seen more flag waving and heard more renditions of "God Bless America" than in the rest of my life combined. There is an incredible outpouring of patriotism and unity in America that is refreshing to see.

As we find our world marching toward the final years of this age, one question we should all want answered is this: Can we do anything to move the heart of God to continue to bless our nation? What can we do as a nation to ensure the continued favor of God upon us as a people?

The answer is really quite simple: We can continue

to experience God's favor as a nation by following God's prescription for national blessing. Three keys to national blessing are set forth in Scripture. We might call these three keys "Biblical Civics 101." We would be wise as a nation, and as individuals, to follow these guidelines.

FATHER ABRAHAM

The first biblical key to national blessing is blessing the Jewish people. All the way back in Genesis 12:3, God made an amazing promise to Abraham and his descendants that has never been revoked: "I will bless those who bless you, and the one who curses you I will curse."

America has consistently been Israel's chief ally. Though we have committed many grievous sins as a nation, we have been a consistent friend of the Jews and the nation of Israel. I believe this is one of the key reasons why God has blessed our nation so greatly throughout our history.

As Charles Ryrie observes:

History has verified this principle. Blessing has often been the lot of individuals and nations who have treated Abraham and the Jewish people kindly. On the other hand, anti-Semitism has been punished by some kind of judgment from God. As we have seen, God is not through with the Jewish people, and therefore He carefully watches to see how individuals and nations treat them today.

So far the United States has received good marks on God's report card in dealing with the Jews. Abraham's descendants have fared well in America. Anti-Semitism has never been strong. The United States was one of the first countries to recognize the State of Israel in 1948. Much of the money needed to sustain that state has come from the United States government or from prosperous American Jews.[34]

Of course, this doesn't mean that as individuals or as a nation we have to agree with or condone everything that Israel does. Some of the decisions the Israeli government makes are unjust and should be opposed. However, we must never be anti-Semitic or place ourselves in a position that is actively hostile to the Jewish people. Rather, we should continue to look for ways to bless the Jews and their nation.

THE BEAUTIFUL PEOPLE

The second biblical key to national blessing is faithfully sharing the Good News of salvation with a needy world. God made the ultimate sacrifice by sending His dear Son to die on the cross for ungodly sinners. This is the good news—that Jesus died in our place on the cross, paying the penalty for our sins, and that He rose again on the third day.

Romans 10:15 reveals the heart of God toward those who take His precious gospel to the lost: "HOW BEAUTIFUL ARE THE FEET OF THOSE WHO BRING GOOD NEWS OF GOOD THINGS!" We don't often think of feet as the most beautiful part of our bodies, but God says that feet that spread the Good News are beautiful. Those who have a part in spreading the Good News to a needy world are beautiful in the sight of God.

I believe a key ingredient in God's blessing on our nation is our active promotion and support of the gospel around the globe. No other nation even comes close to America in terms of the number of people who have personally taken the Good News to the world and who have financed these missions efforts. This is beautiful to God, and He blesses it.

RIGHTEOUSNESS EXALTS A NATION

The third and final way we can invoke the blessing of God upon our nation is by being just, or practicing righteousness in our own lives and promoting righteousness in the society at large. We need to be reminded that the fate of a nation is not ultimately dependent upon politics, military might, or economics, but on righteousness, goodness, and mercy.

Psalm 33:12 says, "Blessed is the nation whose God is the LORD." Proverbs 14:34 is crystal clear: "Righteousness exalts a nation, but sin is a disgrace to any people." And Psalm 9:17 states the promise negatively: "The wicked will return to Sheol, even all the nations who forget God."

One important way for us to continue to experience the outpouring of God's blessing is to elect godly leaders, pray for them (see 1 Timothy 2:1–2), support and vote for government policies that are righteous and good, speak out and vote against government policies and actions that are unrighteous and harmful, and practice holiness in our own lives.

CONCLUSION

As we have seen, there are no direct prophecies about America in the Bible. The most logical explanation for this is that the Rapture will render America a second-rate nation, and she will end up as a part of Antichrist's Western coalition after the Rapture.

However, in the meantime we must never forget these three important lessons for ourselves and our nation: We must (1) be good to the Jewish people and Israel, (2) be actively involved in spreading the gospel to the whole world, and (3) do all we can to practice and promote righteousness in our neighborhoods, cities, states, and in our nation at large.

This will please the Father and secure His continued blessing upon us as a people.

THE MIDNIGHT HOUR

In 1947, scientists created something called the Doomsday Clock to symbolically show how close they believed the world was to a nuclear holocaust.

The hands on this clock have been pushed back and forth sixteen times since 1947. In 1953, amid times of great uncertainty and fear, the hands were set at 11:58 P.M. after the U.S. tested a hydrogen bomb.

On November 27, 1991, the cover of the *Bulletin of the Atomic Scientists* showed the hands on the clock pushed back to 11:43 P.M., their farthest point from "nuclear midnight" since 1947. The reason for this optimism was stated in an accompanying editorial.

"The Cold War is over. The 40-year-long East-West nuclear arms race has ended."[35]

But in May 1998, after India and Pakistan set off nuclear blasts, the hands were advanced to 11:51 P.M.

Although man has his clock signaling the end of the world, we need to remember that God has a timepiece, too, and no one except God knows how close the hands on *His* clock are to midnight.

What if God's "doomsday clock" were to strike midnight today? Are you ready for the coming of the Lord Jesus? Will you be left behind? Do you know for sure where you stand with the Lord?

CHILDLIKE FAITH

You can be prepared for the Rapture (or your death, whichever comes first) by trusting Jesus Christ as your personal Savior from sin. The Bible calls this being "born again" (John 3:7) or being "saved" (see Titus 3:5).

In His mercy, God has made salvation from sin and judgment very simple. In fact, it is so simple that many people stumble over the simplicity. God says that we must become like a child to enter heaven (see Matthew 18:1–3).

You must believe and accept three basic things to have your sins forgiven. First, you must recognize that you are a sinner. That means you admit that you have done things that have offended a perfect and holy God, that you have broken His laws and commandments. Romans 3:23 tells us that we have *all* sinned and come short of the glory of God. Just think, it took only one sin for Adam and Eve to be excluded from the Garden of Eden forever. And it takes only one sin to keep a sinner out of heaven forever.

Second, you must admit that you need a Savior. No matter how much good you may have done in your life, you cannot get rid of your sins. That's a God-sized debt that can only be forgiven by Him. You cannot save yourself. You need a Savior.

Third, you must believe that Jesus Christ is the Savior you need. You must believe that He died for you on the cross and then rose from the dead. And you must receive and accept Him by faith (see John 1:12–13).

There are no magical words or magical prayers that will bring salvation, but the following prayer can serve as a guide if you want to turn to Christ right now. If you truly mean these words as you pray them, you will receive eternal life right where you are (see John 3:36). Will you feel it? Probably not. That's why it's called salvation by faith: You just have to believe that it's a transaction that has taken place if you really meant it. If you're ready, pray something like this:

> Lord, I admit that I am a sinner. I have gone my own way in life and have broken Your laws and commands. I recognize that I cannot save myself by my own good works. I must have a Savior. And I believe that Jesus Christ is the Savior who died for me on the Cross and rose again. I now ask Him to forgive my sins, make me clean, and come into my heart. I trust in Him alone for salvation from sin and for eternal life. Amen.

DON'T PUT IT OFF ANY LONGER

If you want to be prepared for what the future holds—for you personally and for America—pray that prayer right now and receive Jesus Christ as your Savior. God promises us that "WHOEVER WILL CALL ON THE NAME OF THE LORD WILL BE SAVED" (Romans 10:13). Call on Him in faith right now! Put your hand in His, like a little child would, and trust Him with your eternal salvation. It's the best decision you will ever make.

Don't wait! The Rapture may come at any moment.

FOUR KEY QUESTIONS AND ANSWERS ABOUT AMERICA IN THE LAST DAYS

Any discussion of America in Bible prophecy always raises many questions. I hope this book has answered some of yours, but I'm sure it has raised others. Here are a few questions that I commonly hear regarding America in the end times. I hope these answers will help you understand this subject more thoroughly.

1. Is it legitimate for American Christians to rely on 2 Chronicles 7:14 as a formula for national revival and restoration?

It is very common today to hear American Christians refer to 2 Chronicles 7:14 and apply it to our nation. We hear this verse quoted in churches, on the National Day of Prayer, and during times of prayer for national revival and restoration.

> "If my people, who are called by my name, will humble themselves and pray and seek my face and turn from their wicked ways, then will I hear from heaven and will forgive their sin and will heal their land." (NIV)

Second Chronicles 7:14 is God's promise to King Solomon of Israel that anytime the people of Israel find themselves under divine discipline for disobedience and humbly call upon the Lord, He will hear from heaven and heal their land. From the context it is clear that "my people" refers to Israel and that "their land" refers to the land of Israel. This verse is basically a concise reiteration of the conditions for national blessing set forth in God's covenant with Israel in Deuteronomy 28.

The next verse makes this even clearer: "Now My

eyes will be open and My ears attentive to the prayer offered in this place" (v. 15). The place where the prayer is offered is the temple in Jerusalem. Obviously, believers in America are not the nation of Israel, our land is not the Promised Land in Israel, and we don't offer prayer for our nation from the temple mount in Jerusalem.

For these reasons, I do not believe it is legitimate for believers today to directly claim 2 Chronicles 7:14 as a promise for national revival and restoration in America. Having said that, however, I do believe that there are clear points in 2 Chronicles 7:14 that we can and should *apply* to our lives today.

We do this all the time with Old Testament passages of Scripture that don't directly address our situation: After we interpret the passage and discover its meaning in context, we then look for the timeless truth in the passage that God would have us apply to our lives. After all, the Bible tells us: "All Scripture is inspired by God and profitable for teaching, for reproof, for correction, for training in righteousness; so that the man of God may be adequate, equipped for every good work" (2 Timothy 3:16–17).

I believe the timeless truth for us to apply from 2 Chronicles 7:14 is that God desires obedience and humility in His people and that when we come to Him in that way, He hears our cry and brings blessing. God wants His people who are called by His name to continually be humble, seek His face, and be obedient to His Word. If we will faithfully do this, we can be assured that God will bring blessing to us and through us to our community and nation.

2. Will U.S. political efforts successfully bring peace to the Middle East?

Ever since I can remember, the Middle East has been in turmoil, and Israel has been in the eye of the hurricane: the Six-Day War in 1967, the Yom Kippur War in 1973, the war with Lebanon in 1982, the *intifada* (Arabic for "uprising") of 1987, and the Palestinian intifada that began on September 27, 2000.

Peace in the Middle East is the most pursued, most treasured prize in international diplomacy. American presidential administration after administration has taken its crack at solving the Middle East mess. The center of the problem is the chronic, thorny Israeli-Palestinian issue.

I'll never forget the Camp David Accords between Israel and Egypt brokered by President Jimmy Carter in 1978. And who could forget the handshake between Yasser Arafat and Yitzhak Rabin on the White House lawn in front of President Clinton on September 13, 1993? The president and secretary of state are working right now to create a separate, sovereign Palestinian state to bring resolution to the perpetual discord between the Israelis and Palestinians.

But try as they may, no diplomat, secretary, or president will be able to bring lasting peace to the Middle East. The Bible says that peace will come to the Middle East only when the Lord Jesus sets His feet back on this earth to rule and reign.

However, before the true Christ returns to bring real peace, the false Christ will establish his counterfeit kingdom and bring a three-and-a-half-year pseudo-peace to Israel. Scripture's first clue as to the identity of Antichrist is found in Daniel 9:27, where he is pictured brokering a treaty with Israel. "And he [Antichrist] will make a firm covenant with the many

[Israel] for one week [seven years]." When the world gets its first glimpse of Antichrist, he will appear to be a great peacemaker.

The signing of this covenant is one of the most important end-times events predicted in the Bible because it introduces the world to the Antichrist and begins the countdown of the final seven years of this age.

What is the exact nature of this covenant that Antichrist will make with Israel? Charles Dyer, a respected prophecy teacher and author, says:

> What is this "covenant" that the Antichrist will make with Israel? Daniel does not specify its content, but he does indicate that it will extend for seven years. During the first half of this time Israel feels at peace and secure, so the covenant must provide some guarantee for Israel's national security. Very likely the covenant will allow Israel to be at peace with her Arab neighbors. One result of the covenant is that Israel will be allowed to rebuild her temple in Jerusalem. This world ruler will succeed

where Kissinger, Carter, Reagan, Bush, and other world leaders have failed. He will be known as the man of peace![36]

It's interesting that in recent years the Arabs and Israelis are looking more and more to Europe as the mediator to bring peace to the region. This is exactly what the Bible predicts in Daniel 9:27.

After Antichrist, the leader of Europe, brokers this peace deal, all will go along just fine until the midpoint of the seven years. Then the Antichrist will break his treaty with Israel, invade the land, desecrate the rebuilt temple in Jerusalem by setting up an image of himself in the holy of holies, and proclaim himself god. This event will touch off the final three and a half years of this age, the so-called Great Tribulation (see Matthew 24:21).

The world will then endure a time of horror unlike any it has ever known. The only hope for peace in the Middle East and the entire world will be the Prince of Peace, the Lord Jesus Christ, who will return in great power and glory to subdue His enemies and inaugurate His worldwide kingdom. Then, and only then, will peace come to the Middle East and the rest of the world.

However, the fact that lasting peace in the Middle East won't happen until Christ comes should not deter us from doing all we can as a people and nation to stop further bloodshed in Israel and the Middle East. We should support and pray for our government leaders who are doing the best they can to bring some resolution to the problems in that part of the world and in every part of the world that suffers violence, bloodshed, and conflict.

3. Could the Antichrist come from the United States?

According to Scripture, the coming Antichrist will be a Gentile (i.e. a non-Jew) who will rule the world for three and a half years. Since America is the most powerful nation in the world, people often ask if the Antichrist could come from the United States, or even if he could be a U.S. president.

Daniel 9:26 tells us that the Antichrist will be of the same nationality as the people who destroyed the Jewish temple in A.D. 70. Since we know that the Romans destroyed the temple, we can also know that the Antichrist will be of Roman origin. He will rise out of the reunited Roman Empire

Most people have taken this to mean that he will come out of one of the nations of Europe that formed the nucleus of the old Roman Empire, possibly even from the city of Rome itself. However, since the United States came from European nations that once constituted the Roman Empire and has language and laws derived from Rome, is it possible that the Antichrist could come from America? Could he even be an American president?

No one can say for sure. Although he could be an American, it seems best to believe that the Antichrist will come out of Europe. This was the Roman Empire that existed in John's day when he prophesied Antichrist's coming from a future form of the Roman Empire. (Compare Daniel 7:7–8 with Revelation 13:1–4 and 17:11–13.)

However, regardless of where he comes from, one thing is sure: He is coming, and he will do exactly what the Bible predicts.

4. Will troops from the United States be at Armageddon?

We can confidently say that the United States will participate in Armageddon. Two main points support this conclusion. First, Scripture indicates that all the nations of the world will be gathered against Israel at Armageddon:

- Zechariah 12:3: "'It will come about in that day that I will make Jerusalem a heavy stone for all the peoples; all who lift it will be severely injured. And all the nations of the earth will be gathered against it.'"
- Zechariah 14:2: "For I will gather all the nations against Jerusalem to battle, and the city will be captured, the houses plundered, the women ravished and half of the city exiled, but the rest of the people will not be cut off from the city."
- Revelation 16:14: "For they are spirits of demons, performing signs, which go out to the kings of the whole world, to gather them together for the war of the great day of God, the Almighty."

This does not mean that every nation currently in existence will be at Armageddon, since the face of the world may change drastically between now and then. However, it does mean that the United States—in whatever form it is in at that time—will invade Israel with all the rest of the world at Armageddon.

The second reason I believe that American troops will participate in Armageddon is that we know that Antichrist will lead the West in its invasion of Israel at the end of the Tribulation. Since I have concluded that America will be part of Antichrist's Western empire in the end times, it follows that America will participate in the events of Armageddon.

Today, America is Israel's chief ally and protector. But in the end times, even America will join Antichrist and turn against Israel and the Jewish people.

NOTES

1. Charles C. Ryrie, *The Best Is Yet to Come* (Chicago: MoodyPress, 1981), 109.
2. This story was taken from *Heaven Help Us* by Steven J. Lawson (Colorado Springs, Colo.: NavPress, 1995), 99–100.
3. Ryrie, *The Best Is Yet to Come,* 106.
4. Thomas Ice and Timothy Demy, *The Truth about America in the Last Days* (Eugene, Ore.: Harvest House, 1998), 7.
5. S. Franklin Logsdon, *Is the U.S.A. in Prophecy?* (Grand Rapids, Mich.: Zondervan, 1968), 9.
6. Ibid., 59–60. Note that Logsdon's work was published in 1968, during the height of the cold war between the U.S. and the Soviet Union. Edward Tracy's book, *The United States in Prophecy,* supports Logsdon's thesis that the United States is the Babylon of the end times. Edward Tracy, *The United States in Prophecy* (Pine Grove, Calif.: Convale Publications, 1969).

7. Jack Van Impe, *The Great Escape* (Nashville, Tenn.: Word, 1998), 207.

8. Jack Van Impe, *2001: On the Edge of Eternity* (Nashville, Tenn.: Word, 1996), 179.

9. Paraphrased from R. A. Coombes, *America, the Babylon: America's Destiny Foretold in Biblical Prophecy* (Liberty, Mo.: REAL Publishing, 1998), 55–8.

10. Ibid., 182–6. Also paraphrased.

11. Ibid., 132.

12. Charles H. Dyer, *The Rise of Babylon* (Wheaton, Ill.: Tyndale, 1991), 182.

13. Robert Thomas, *Revelation 8–22* (Chicago: Moody Press, 1995), 307.

14. Charles H. Dyer, "The Identity of Babylon in Revelation 17–18," *Bibliotheca Sacra* 144 (October– December 1987): 441–3.

15. Van Impe, *The Great Escape,* 206.

16. E. F. Webber, *America in Prophecy* (Oklahoma City, Okla.: Southwest Radio Church, 1993), 6. Webber lists eight points from Isaiah 18:1–2 that he believes identify the United States as this unnamed nation.

17. Geoffrey W. Grogan, "Isaiah," in *The Expositor's Bible Commentary*, ed. Frank E. Gaebelein (Grand Rapids, Mich.: Zondervan, 1986), 6:122.

18. Wilhelm Gesenius, *Gesenius' Hebrew and Chaldee*

Lexicon, trans. Samuel Prideaux Tregelles (Grand Rapids, Mich.: Wm. B. Eerdmans, 1949), 752.

19. Ed Hindson, *Is the Antichrist Alive and Well?* (Eugene, Ore.: Harvest House, 1998), 127.

20. Van Impe, *2001: On the Edge of Eternity,* 178.

21. David Allen Lewis, *Prophecy 2000* (Green Forest, Ark.: New Leaf Press, 1990), 101, 103.

22. Tim LaHaye, "Is the United States in Bible Prophecy?" *National Liberty Journal* 26 (February 1997): 16.

23. John F. Walvoord, *The Nations in Prophecy* (Grand Rapids, Mich.: Zondervan, 1967), 175.

24. Ibid., 172.

25. Barna Research Online, "American Faith Is Diverse, as Shown among Five Faith-Based Segments," 29 January 2002. http://www.barna.org/cgibin/PagePressRelease.asp?PressReleaseID=105& Reference=C.

26. Though there are certainly nonevangelicals and Catholics who are true believers in Christ—not to mention some who claim to be evangelicals who are not true believers—I have chosen to use these statistics because they provide at least a general picture of the spiritual landscape in various nations and the effect that the Rapture will have when it occurs. See Patrick Johnstone, *Operation World,* 4th ed. (Grand Rapids, Mich.: Zondervan, 1987).

27. I believe that the small children of Christians will be raptured alongside of their believing parents.

28. Patrick Johnstone, *Operation World,* 4th ed. (Grand Rapids, Mich.: Zondervan, 1987), 34.

29. John Henry Nosen, "Is Europe the Forgotten Mission Field?" WorldBase Norway, 1.

30. Dyer, *The Rise of Babylon,* 168.

31. Ryrie, *The Best Is Yet to Come,* 110–11. Many others support this same view. See Hindson, *Is the Antichrist Alive and Well?* 127–8; Arno Froese, "United Europe's Power Play," in *Foreshocks of Antichrist,* ed. William T. James (Eugene, Ore.: Harvest House, 1997), 284–7. J. Dwight Pentecost, *Prophecy for Today* (Grand Rapids, Mich.:Discovery House Publishers, 1989), 104.

32. Ed Dobson, *The End* (Grand Rapids, Mich.: Zondervan, 1997), 167.

33. Walvoord, *The Nations in Prophecy,* 173.

34. Ryrie, *The Best Is Yet to Come,* 111–2.

35. Mike Moore, "A New Era," *Bulletin of the Atomic Scientists,* December 1991. http://www.bullatomicsci.org/issues/1991/d91/d91ed.html (accessed 13 December 2001).

36. Charles H. Dyer, *World News and Bible Prophecy* (Wheaton, Ill.: Tyndale, 1995), 214.

END TIMES ANSWERS

WHAT ON EARTH IS GOING ON?

Pierce through the post-9/11 clouds of sensationalism and skepticism with prophecy expert Mark Hitchcock as he gives a balanced view of today's major global developments signaling Christ's return.
ISBN 1-57673-853-1

IS AMERICA IN BIBLE PROPHECY?

Will America suffer a great fall? Find out what's in store for the world's superpower in the coming days with prophecy scholar and pastor Mark Hitchcock.
ISBN 1-57673-496-X

THE COMING ISLAMIC INVASION OF ISRAEL

Mark Hitchcock shows how events today may be setting the stage for the fulfillment of Ezekiel's prediction—a Russian-Islamic confederation of nations will finally invade Israel and be destroyed by God.
ISBN 1-59052-048-3

IS THE ANTICHRIST ALIVE TODAY?

Is the Antichrist alive today, right now, in this generation? Prophecy expert Mark Hitchcock discusses five current events preparing the world for the Antichrist's reign.
ISBN 1-59052-075-0

SEVEN SIGNS OF THE END TIMES

Are you noticing the symptoms of the end of the world? Get an expert opinion. Find out seven specific signs the Bible says to look for.
ISBN 1-59052-129-3

101 ANSWERS TO THE MOST ASKED QUESTIONS ABOUT THE END TIMES

The end is near! Or is it? The Antichrist is alive and well today! *Or is he?* The church is about to be raptured and will certainly escape the Tribulation...*right?* When it comes to the end times, there's so much confusion. Preachers with elaborate charts share their theories about Revelation and other prophetic books of the Bible. "Ah, Babylon stands for the United States," they say. But then other teachers share their theories: "No, Babylon stands for the Roman Catholic Church, or the European Union, or the literal Babylon rebuilt in Iraq...." *Would somebody please shoot straight with me?* Finally, someone has. Gifted scholar and pastor Mark Hitchcock walks you gently through Bible prophecy in an engaging, user-friendly style. Hitchcock's careful examination of the topic will leave you feeling informed and balanced in your understanding of events to come...in our time?

ISBN 1-57673-952-X

THE SECOND COMING OF BABYLON

Stirrings in Iraq—Is Babylon Back? The Bible says that Babylon will be rebuilt and become the economic center of the world. Even now the ruins of the ancient city—just sixty miles south of Baghdad, Iraq—are quietly stirring. What does it mean for America? For Israel? For every person alive today? Are we living in the last days of earth as we know it? Find out, from Bible prophecy expert Mark Hitchcock...

- How the focus of the world will shift back to Babylon
- How Antichrist will make Babylon his capital
- How the kingdoms of earth will fade as Babylon rises
- The false powers of Antichrist will grow
- How prophecy will be fulfilled—and Babylon finally destroyed!

ISBN 1-59052-251-6